AF865235

Bleeds & Margins

The Whitebook Series:

*Build Your Book:**—XXX pages, color, Instructions on how to convert a Word or OpenOffice document into a book suitable for printing by most print-on-demand companies, with particular focus on CreateSpace.

*CS Digital—Bleeds & Margins:** 48 pages, color. Lists the complete CreateSpace submission guidelines with illustrated explanations of most common problems dealing with them. ISBN 978-0615588018. $14.95

CS Digital Sampler: 42 pages, color. Shows how CreateSpace prints color, full uploaded PDF available free to enable comparing the source file to the printed piece and comparing your monitor and printer to what CS prints.ISBN 978-0615587813. $12.95

Prepress Glossary:* 80 pages, color. 350 definitions, illustrated, with articles on color, file formats, grayscale, paper, PDFs, resolution, and transparency, and over two dozen notes uniquely relevant to CreateSpace users. ISBN 978-0615591599. $22.95

Quick Guide to Mechanics & Punctuation: 40 pages, black and white. A quick guide to italicization, capitalization, syllabication, numbers, block quotes, punctuation (US), and prepositions and conjunctions. ISBN 978-0615587967. $6.95

Type & Typography—Part 1:* 79 pages, black and white; 48 pages on typography and a 28 page, 350 illustrated-definition glossary of type and typographic terms. ISBN 978-0615749495. $8.95

Type & TypographyC—Part 2:* 416 pages, black and white. A type book of type specimens for 2,954 fonts, over 90% of which are free, commercial use fonts readily available on line. ISBN 978-0615749501. $24.95

*These books will be part of *The Giant Book of Print on Demand* (working title),800+ pages, black and white, due out spring, 2013.

Whitebook Series

CS Digital—Bleeds &Margins

Guide to CreateSpace Submission Guidelines

Walton Mendelson

December, 2012
One-Off Press

CS Digital—Bleeds & Margins is part of a larger book, *The Giant Book of Print-on-Demand* (working title), due out this spring, 2013. This, and other sections, are being printed in color, inasmuch as most of the diagrams and illustrations benefit from being in color. The larger book, because of its size, 800+ pages, will be in black and white.

Thanks to Michelle Lovi and Steve Johnson for reviewing an early draft of this book. All mistakes and errors in this edition, are the sole fault of the author.

ISBN 978-0615588018

Table of Contents

CreateSpace Guidelines

The goal of *Bleeds & Margins* is to expand upon CS's simplistic submission guidelines. These guidelines were most recently downloaded November 12, 2012.

Periodically, CS changes its submission guidelines. It is highly recommended that you check what is current before formatting your book.

The basis for the interpretation that follows is based on working on books printed through Book-Surge and later CreateSpace since 2003, on several years of giving active support in the CS forum, and working with clients designing, formatting, and submitting books and covers to CS. Some things also came from conversations and email communications with Tech and Customer Support people.

Pages 7-14: Quoted verbatim. Footnotes and notes that are not part the CS web pages are in gray boxes.

COVER*

Note: All covers are printed in full color—black and white covers are printed in color—and are included in the per book cost. All covers are laminiated.

❶ Calculate the spine width of your book

The spine width is based on the number of pages in your book:

For black and white-interior books:

White paper: multiply page count by 0.002252

Cream paper: multiply page count by 0.0025

Example of spine width calculation for a 60-page black and white book printed on white paper: 60 x 0.002252 = 0.135"

For color-interior books:

Multiply page count by 0.002347

Example of spine width calculation for a 60-page color book: 60 x 0.002347 = 0.141"

❷ Set up your document

Your cover must be a single PDF that includes the back cover, spine, and front cover as one image. You can submit your cover on any size page as long as the printable area is:

- Measured exactly to your book's trim size, spine width, and .125" bleed
- Centered horizontally and vertically

Minimum Cover Width: Bleed + Back Cover Trim Size + Spine Width + Front Cover Trim Size + Bleed

Example calculation at 6" x 9" cover with 60 B&W pages on white paper: 0.125" + 6" + 0.135" + 6" + .125" = 12.385"

* Emphasis (e.g. bold) and spacing have been changed to make theses pages clearer in print.

Minimum Cover Height: Bleed + Book Height Trim Size + Bleed
Example calculation: 6" x 9": 0.125" + 9" + .125" = 9.25"

Get a head start with one of our cover templates: Our templates make it easier for you to quickly create print-ready files in Adobe Photoshop®, Adobe InDesign®, or any software that will allow you to open a .png or PDF file and save a PDF file. These templates contain the proper dimensions, layout, and bleed for the trim size and page count you select. Download Cover Templates: https://www.createspace.com/Help/Book/Artwork.do

❸ Design your cover*

Note: All covers are presumed to bleed. The cover art must extend to at least 0.125" beyond the trim line on all four sides—even if it is white.

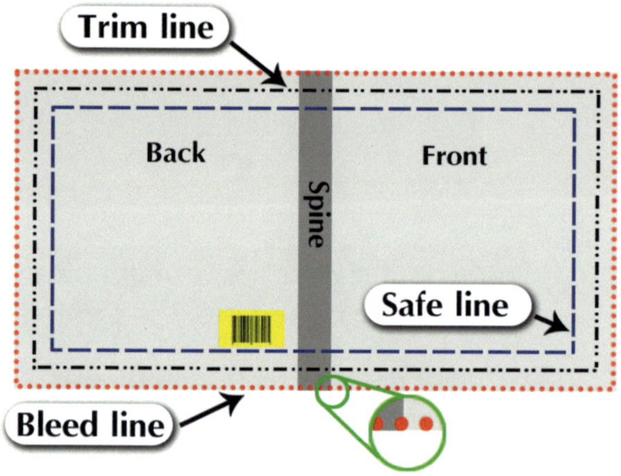

Safe Zone: Text and images must be at least .125" inside the trim lines to ensure that no live elements are cut during the bookmaking process.

Title and Author Name: Your book's title and the author's name must appear on the cover exactly as it was entered during the title setup process.

Images: Images may be CMYK or RGB color. All images should be sized at 100%, flattened to one layer and placed in your document at a minimum resolution of 300 DPI.

The spine of your book: Every book will vary slightly when bound. Allow for 0.0625" variance on either side of the fold lines for your cover. For example, if your spine width is 1", your text should be no wider than 0.875". Because of this variance, avoid hard edges or lines that end on the fold line.

For books with 130 pages or less, we strongly recommend a blank spine. Blank spines are required for books with less than 101 pages.

Barcode:† When your files go through the review process, our system will place your ISBN barcode in a 2" by 1.2" white box in the lower right-hand corner of your book's back cover. Our standard trim size templates will show you exact barcode placement.

Images or text in the barcode location will be covered when the book is printed. Make sure no important elements appear where the barcode will be placed.
If you choose to provide and place your own barcode, be sure it is a high-resolution image.

❹ Prepare for Printing

* I redrew this diagram for this book. The original is vague regarding what things are and how they are to be interpreted or used.
† See page 48.

1. The printable area of your document must be the right size, including bleed.
2. Make sure the printable area is centered within your document.
3. Make sure all live elements are inside the safe zone.
4. Export your file (https://www.createspace.com/en/community/docs/DOC-1331) as a print-ready PDF. Be sure fonts are embedded.
5. The maximum accepted file size for your book cover is 40 MB.
   <https://www.createspace.com/Products/Book/CoverPDF.jsp> 12 November 2012

INTERIOR

❶ Set up your Document

One text-page per PDF-page; One PDF-page per page number. Your document's dimensions will be the book's final trim size, plus bleed (optional) with margins.

Note: Each sheet of hinged paper in a book is called a leaf. Each leaf has two sides, and each side is a page—regardless of whether the page is numbered or not.

Trim Size This is the final cut-size of your book in width by height. Learn more about choosing a trim size [see next page]

Margins

Gutter margins are by the book's binding. You'll want a wider margin for longer (thicker) books. See the table for what to set your inside margins to.

Page Count	Inside Margin	Outside Margins
24 to 150 pages	.375"	at least .25"
151 to 400 pages	.75"	at least .25"
401 to 600 pages	.875"	at least .25"
More than 600 pages	1.0"	at least .25"

Outside margins are the page edges opposite of the binding, and the top and bottom margins. All live text and images must have an outside margin of at least .25"—but we recommend an outside margin of at least .5"

Note: In Programs like Word, the margins are set to Mirror margins. Instead of left and right, each page has an inside and outside margin, which are relative to book spread. "Gutter" is a misued word. Except for column (the column gutter), ignore the gutter setting (set to 0").

Does your book contain images?*

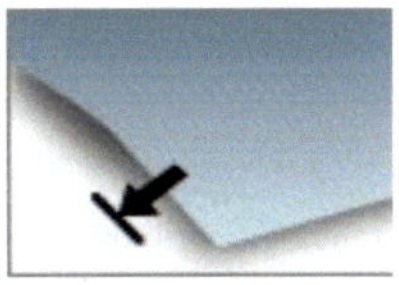

If you want your images to bleed to the edges of your book, ensure that they extend at least .125" beyond the final trim size from the top, bottom and outer edges and submit your PDF .25" higher and .125" wider than your selected trim size to accommodate the full bleed area.

Keep in mind all live elements must be at least .25" away from the trim lines, so if your file is formatted to be full bleed all live elements should be .375" away from the edge of the page.

Note: if your art is on a white background, the edge of the white background must be 0.25" away from the trim lines: i.e. not in the out-of-live margin.

* See page 15 & 48 for tips on working with images.

❷ Design and format your content

Title and Author Name: Your book's title and the author's name must appear exactly as it was entered during our title setup process.

Images: Images may be CMYK or RGB color. All images should be sized at 100%, flattened to one layer and placed in your document at a minimum resolution of 300 DPI.

❸ Checklist: Prepare for Printing

1. Make sure the dimensions of your document match your trim size (including bleed if applicable).
2. Make sure all live elements are within the proper margins or safe zone.
3. Export your file as a print-ready PDF. Be sure fonts are embedded.
4. The maximum accepted file size for your book interior is 400 MB.

Additional Notes*

An additional page with a manufacturing-related barcode is added to the back of all books. Books may also have blank pages at the end. Neither the barcode nor the additional pages may be eliminated.

<https://www.createspace.com/Products/Book/InteriorPDF.jsp> 12 November 2012

BLEED

Bleed refers to how images are positioned within your book.

- If you do not want a margin around the outside edge of each page with an image, you'll need to format your images with extra variance and select the bleed option:
- Make sure that all images extend at least .125" from each top, bottom, and outer edge beyond the final trim size.
- Submit your PDF .25" higher and .125" wider than your selected trim size to accommodate the full bleed area.
- Account for variance by keeping all live elements (essential text and images that should not be trimmed) at least .25" away from the trim lines.
- Images cannot bleed across the middle of the book without a small white line in the book's gutter.
- If all your images are placed within a margin of at least .25" on every page, do not select the bleed option.

<Pop-up note from link regarding bleeds>

TRIM

Choose a Trim Size

Remember to consider Expanded Distribution channels before selecting a trim size.

Learn more about trim size requirements for each Expanded Distribution channel.

Information about industry standard trim sizes for black and white and full color books is included in the tables below.

* On the web page, there is a link to interior templates. These are not consistently good, and some people have more troubles with them than they are worth. They do make reasonably good models to follow to set up your own files, but I cannot recommend them.

Note: CS can print any books size between:
4″ x 6″ to 8.5″ x 11.69″
The minimum height is 6″ and the maximum width is 8.5″. Thus, for books with the binding on the left, square to landscape to square could be within:
6″ x 6″ to 8.5″ x 8.5″

Black and White Books

Trim Size	White Paper Page Count	Cream Paper Page Count	Ind. Std.
5 x 8 inches * 12.7 x 20.32 centimeters	24 - 828	24 - 740	✓
5.06 x 7.81 inches * 12.9 x 19.8 centimeters	24 - 828	24 - 740	✓
5.25 x 8 inches * 13.335 x 20.32 centimeters	24 - 828	24 - 740	✓
5.5 x 8.5 inches * 13.97 x 21.59 centimeters 2	24 - 828	24 - 740	✓
6 x 9 inches * 15.24 x 22.86 centimeters	24 - 828	24 - 740	✓
6.14 x 9.21 inches * 15.6 x 23.4 centimeters	24 - 828	24 - 740	✓
6.69 x 9.61 inches * 17 x 24.4 centimeters	24 - 828	24 - 740	✓
7 x 10 inches * 17.78 x 25.4 centimeters	24 - 828	24 - 740	✓
7.44 x 9.69 inches* 18.9 x 24.6 centimeters	24 - 828	24 - 740	✓
7.5 x 9.25 inches * 19.1 x 23.5 centimeters	24 - 828	24 - 740	✓
8 x 10 inches * 20.32 x 25.4 centimeters	24 - 440	24-400	✓
8.25 x 6 inches * 20.955 x 15.24 centimeters	24-220	24-200	
8.25 x 8.25 inches 20.955 x 20.955 centimeters	24-220	24-200	
8.5 x 8.5 inches * 21.59 x 21.59 centimeters	24-630	24-570	
8.5 x 11 inches * 21.59 x 27.94 centimeters	24-630	24-570	✓

* These sizes (somewhat different between black and white books and color books), marked with an asterisk, are available in hardbound for author purchases only. Hardbound copies are not listed on Amazon or eStore. They are available for a one-time set up fee, currently $99, and an addition per book fee. Consult Customer Service about this feature.

Full-Color Books

Trim Size	White Paper Page Count	Ind. Std.
5 x 8 inches * 12.7 x 20.32 centimeters	24 - 480	
5.06 x 7.81 inches 12.9 x 19.8 centimeters	24 - 480	
5.25 x 8 inches * 13.335 x 20.32 centimeters	24 - 480	
5.5 x 8.5 inches * 13.97 x 21.59 centimeters 2	24 - 480	✓
6 x 9 inches * 15.24 x 22.86 centimeters	24 - 480	✓
6.14 x 9.21 inches 15.6 x 23.4 centimeters	24 - 480	✓
6.69 x 9.61 inches 17 x 24.4 centimeters	24 - 480	
7 x 10 inches * 17.78 x 25.4 centimeters	24 - 480	✓
7.44 x 9.69 inches 18.9 x 24.6 centimeters	24 - 480	
7.5 x 9.25 inches * 19.1 x 23.5 centimeters	24 - 480	
8 x 10 inches* 20.32 x 25.4 centimeters	24 - 480	✓
8.25 x 6 inches * 20.955 x 15.24 centimeters	24-212	
8.25 x 8.25 inches * 20.955 x 20.955 centimeters	24-212	
8.5 x 8.5 inches * 21.59 x 21.59 centimeters	24 - 480	✓
8.5 x 11 inches * 21.59 x 27.94 centimeters	24 - 480	✓

Want to create your own custom trim size? "Enter my own size" trim sizes can be sold on Amazon.com and your eStore, but are ineligible for the Bookstores and Online Retailers channel within Expanded Distribution. [https://www.createspace.com/Products/Book/ExpandedDistribution.jsp]

Note: In addition to the specifications above regarding industry standard sizes and Expanded Distribution options, the choice of ISBN (all books must have an ISBN) also effects these choices (see "What are My ISBN options?" next page).

ISBN

What's an ISBN? An ISBN, or International Standard Book Number, is a unique 10- or 13-digit number assigned to every published book. An ISBN identifies a title's edition, publisher, and physical properties such as trim size, page count, and binding type.

How are ISBNs used? Bookstores, retailers, and libraries identify books by their ISBNs. We print an ISBN barcode on the lower back right corner of every book we manufacture.

What are my ISBN options? You have four ISBN options: you can either use a CreateSpace-Assigned ISBN, a Custom ISBN*, a Custom Universal ISBN*, or you can use your own ISBN. Both custom ISBN options are offered through an agreement with Bowker®.

	Price	Imprint	Distributors
CreateSpace-Assigned ISBN	Free	CreateSpace Independent Publishing Platform	CreateSpace
Custom ISBN*	$10	You choose	Createspace
Custom Universal ISBN*	$99	You choose	You choose
Provide Your Own ISBN	Existing ISBN Required	You choose	You choose

CreateSpace-Assigned ISBN :

- CreateSpace Independent Publishing Platform is your book's imprint of record. If you select Amazon.com or Amazon's European websites as distribution channels, this imprint will be reflected on your book's detail page.
- You can sell your book through Amazon.com, Amazon's European websites, a CreateSpace eStore, and all Expanded Distribution channels.
- This ISBN can only be used with the CreateSpace Independent Publishing Platform.
- Your book's ISBN information will be registered with BooksInPrint.com®

$10 Custom ISBN*

- You choose your book's imprint of record. If you select Amazon.com or Amazon's European websites as distribution channels, this imprint will be reflected on your book's detail page.
- You can sell your book through Amazon.com, Amazon's European websites, a CreateSpace eStore, and some† Expanded Distribution channels.
- This ISBN can only be used with the CreateSpace Independent Publishing Platform.
- Your book's ISBN information will be registered with BooksInPrint.com®

$99 Custom Universal ISBN*

- You can use this ISBN with any publisher.
- You choose your book's imprint of record. If you select Amazon.com or Amazon's European websites as distribution channels, this imprint will be reflected on your book's detail page.

---

* Available to U.S.-based members only. Before purchasing a Custom or Custom Universal ISBN option, you must agree to the Bowker Terms and Conditions

† Not eligible for distribution through the Libraries and Academic Institutions channel.

- You can sell your book through Amazon.com, Amazon's European websites, a CreateSpace eStore, and some† Expanded Distribution channels.
- Your book's ISBN information will be registered with BooksInPrint.com®

Provide Your Own ISBN
- You can purchase your own ISBN from Bowker or through your local ISBN agency.
- If you are reprinting your book, the title, author name, and binding type must remain the same. A new edition requires a new ISBN.
- Your book's imprint must match what's on file with your ISBN.
- You can sell your book through Amazon.com, an eStore, and some† Expanded Distribution channels.

< https://www.createspace.com/Products/Book/ISBNs.jsp> 12 November 2012

Note: 1) While the CS Free ISBN offers the most distribution channels, the effectiveness of these additional channels is arguable. In most on-line discussions, most CS members say they get few if any sales through them; however, there are a few members who sell a lot through them. It is most likely that their effectiveness is related to the author/publisher's marketing approach. 2) Many members simply prefer to have their own imprint—narrowing the choices. 3) If you intend to use other printers then you need to use the Custom Universal ISBN or provide your own (in the US, purchasing a block of ten ISBNs from Bowker is cost effective). 4) Books do not have to be made available commerically: many people publish books only for family, business, etc., and do not enable any of the distribution channels.

PAPER

Color Books: 60# smooth bright white off-set
Black and White:
    White paper: 60# off-set
    Off-white paper: 60# cream off-set
Cover stock: 10pt C1S

60# off-set is the equivalent of 24# bond paper most of us use to print with at home. "Offset paper" is a descriptive label meaning that it is appropriate for off-set printing. The paper for color printing is probably coated (**not** like art books, **not** clay or cast coated) to print color images significantly better than the other papers CS offers. The cover is the equivalent of 65# bond paper. Covers only print one side (no printing on the inside covers), and are laminated.

---

† Not eligible for distribution through the Libraries and Academic Institutions channel.

Warnings

Always have a copy of your file/book/cover in as pristine a file as possible. Keep it safe. Work with copies. Develop a good naming system.

All pages in a book must be the same size and orientation (portrait or landscape); however, the content could be either—if the minimum margins are honored.

Because CS prints from PDFs, it is best if you create your PDF, rather than rely on a CS conversion.

Most PDF conversion programs default to 8.5 x 11. You may have to set the paper/trim/output size to what you want, rather than expect it to be automatically set.

If you upload a Word file, it is preferable to have it in Word 95–2003 (doc), than in the newer docx format.

When sending a Word file to someone for formatting, either send it as a zip file or use a file transfer site/service: there is a kind of file corruption that can happen to Word files when sent as email attachments. This is not common, but Acrobat has an error message about it.

The ideal image resolution is 300 dpi,* higher resolution does nothing unless you are applying it to 1-bit art.

Use insert or place to put images into your document.

Images should be the exact size (length x width @300 dpi) needed before inserting them.

Keep a folder just for the images sized as you need them; keep a separate folder of the images in their original state.

Multilayered images should not be flattened, but saved in their native format with all layers intact. Flatten a copy of the image file for your book.

If you use images in Word files, be aware that Word defaults to "compress" images. "Compress" is Microsoft's word, it is not compression, rather it is downsizing: 300dpi images will be downsized to 200dpi or less (I've seen them downsized to 96dpi).

If you use Word, and you will have images in your book:

Disable image compression before inserting images and before saving the file:

- Word 2010—*File > Options > Advanced > Image size and quality > Do not compress images in this file.*
- Word 2007—*Click an image to bring up the Picture Tools ribbon*
  Click Compress Pictures
  Click options
  Uncheck 'Automatically perfrom basic compression on save'
  Click OK
  Make sure 'Apply to selected pictures only' is unchecked and hit ok

Do not drag and drop images into the file: your images could downsize.

Do not resize the images inside your file: your images will downsize.

Do not use Word's Save as PDF feature: it will downsize your images to 200dpi.

Give your uploads, especially revisions, discrete names: you want to be able to identify them by name in case there is a database problem.

---

* Dpi, dots per inch, is more correctly stated for image resolution as ppi, pixels per inch. Inasmuch as most people use dpi, I will use dpi rather than ppi and then having keep footnoting it with an explanation.

Pages

The trim size of a book is the same as the paper size or output size of your file. CS will not resize your book: when you create the project, the trim size you enter is expected to be the trim size of the book.

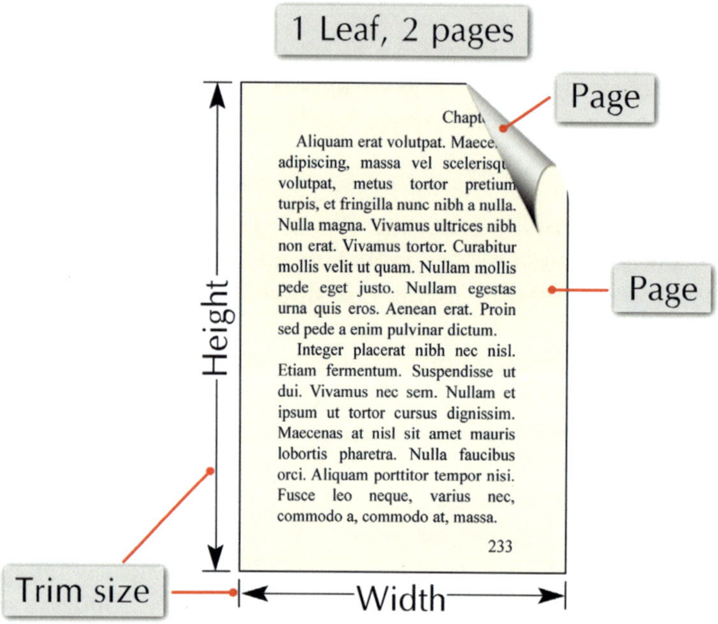

Customarily the width is given before the height: e.g. 6 x 9 denotes a book that trims to 6 inches wide by 9 inches high.

As noted earlier, when determining the minimum inside margin or the width of the spine, CS asks for the total page count, every page in the book is counted, regardless of whether it is numbered or not.*

The following illustration shows a spread—the left and right hand pages. It is labeled "Reader's Spread" because this is how a book spread looks, finished, in a book, to the reader; and to distinguish it from other sorts of spreads. In printing, printer's spreads show the relations of pages as they print, after which they are folded, gathered, and trimmed: they often do not show consecutive pages as a reader would see them. In Word, for example, files start with the first page on the left, with the second page on the right: thus these spreads are reversed, having the odd pages on the left and the right. (OpenOffice/LibreOffice has a book view that does show files in reader's spreads.

To achieve margins suitable for books, some programs, like Word, have to have the margins mirrored. Instead of left and right margins, there is an outside and an inside margin on each page, each relative to the spine of the book.

---

* However, when the page count for a book is given in its bibliographic details, it often excludes some of the front matter. Such a count might start with the full title page, or the copyright page, etc.

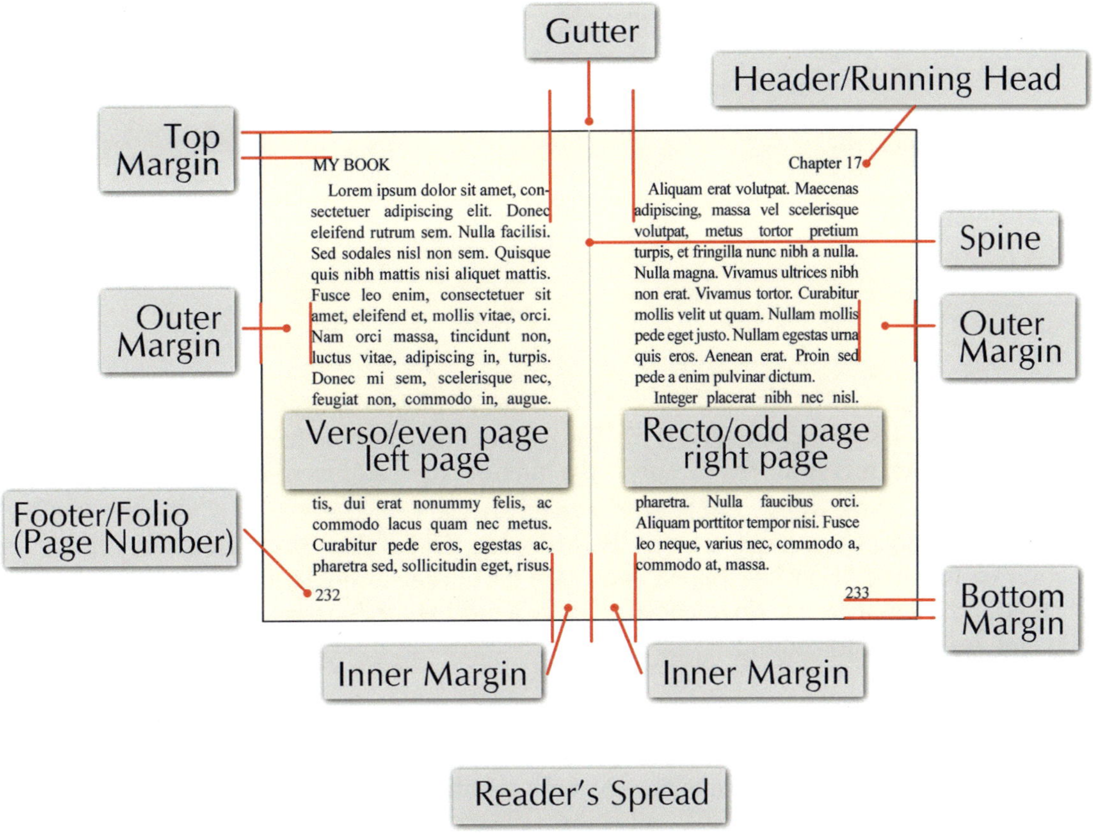

Where most word processors and desktop publishing programs define the top and the bottom margins as the top and bottom of the text block itself, CS defines the top and bottom margins as the distance to any text or image: here it is the distance from the edge of the page to the top of the running heads or the bottom of the folios.

Some programs have a setting for gutter as well as for the inside margin. If you want a 1″ inner margin you could set the gutter to 0.2″ and the inside margin to 0.8″, but this seems silly at best: set the gutter to 0” and the inside margin to 1.0” and it is clear and obvious what you will get.

Note that the CS minimum margins are just that: *minimum* margins. Your margins must meet or exceed them. Most books have significantly bigger margins than the CS minimums, with the exception of the inner margins which are sometimes larger than average. CS uses a tight binding, see page 22, which causes 0.25″ to be lost in the spine edge of the gutter, so the larger inner margins are helpful to the reader. Assume that you will visually, if not physically, lose 0.25″.

In assessing your margins, print out your pages, and, ideally, you'll create spreads that are trimmed to size. Monitors are not reliable—there is too much clutter around the pages.

Bleeds & Margins

Cover Templates: As of summer, 2011, the CS cover templates changed. They now show both the bleed and the no-live element zone* in red. The no-live element zone has also changed from 0.25" to 0.125"; however, this is for covers only—the interior pages still require a 0.25" margin.

Note: the new templates, middle, are on a 19" x 13"white field. If you use the template, you can keep the cover on that field. It can be cropped away, as in the bottom example, and if you create your own cover without a template, you do not need to make it any bigger than the cover art itself: cover plus bleed with no white background.

The written guidelines still say (see page 7) that if a cover is submitted on a canvas larger than the cover itself it should be centered vertically and horizontally. This contradicts the new template, middle. I would suggest either use the template as positioned on the middle example, or cropped as in the bottom.

Cropping, bottom, is the safest way to deal with a cover that is white, which must include a white bleed as well. If the white cover is on a large, oversized white background it is impossible to see where the edges of the cover are, and several members have had their covers wrongly adjusted by CS—which would not have happened if the covers had been cropped to the outside edge of the bleed.

Note: the drop shadow is only a device used here to set off the background. Do not add a drop shadow.

Do not use any printer's marks, e.g. registration or crop marks. CS will reject any print-ready file with them.

Templates are generated in increments of ten pages. For example, if you download a:
296 pg template it will fit a 291–300 page book, and, it will have "300" in the file title.
302 pg template it will fit a 301–310 page book, and, it will have "310" in the file title.
318 pg template it will fit a 311–320 page book, and, it will have "320" in the file title.

---

* This inner zone or margin has had several names: title-safe, no-live element, out-of-live, no-text. "**Live Elements/Graphics** are the content that is placed within the viewable area (or safe zone) of a page that is always seen. Ensuring all elements are contained within this area safeguards that no essential elements are cut during the bookmaking process," Glossary of CreateSpace™ Terms.

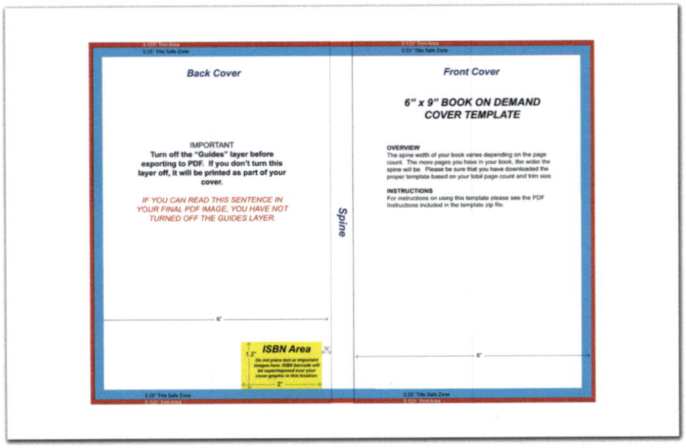

Old, pre-Summer, 2011: 17 x 11 background

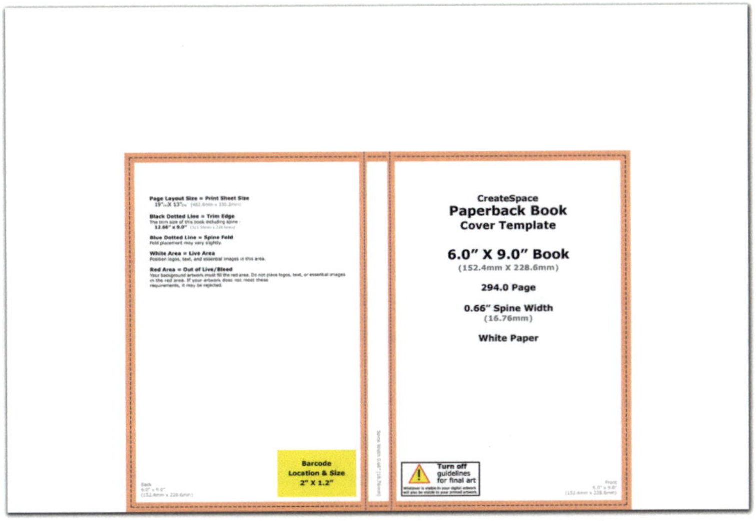

New, 2011: 19 x 13 background

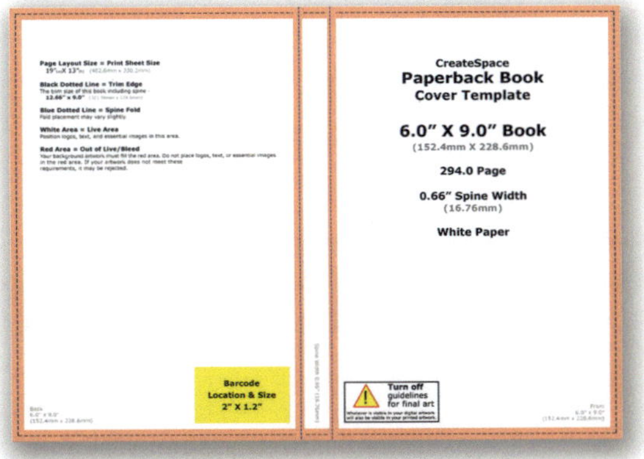

New, 2011: cropped to size

Cover Templates: As of summer, 2011, the CS cover templates changed. They now show both the bleed and the no-live element zone* in red. The no-live element zone has also changed from 0.25" to 0.125"; however, this is for covers only—the interior pages still require a 0.25" margin.

This new template† also shows that text on the spine:

- may only be used on books over 101 pages
- is recommended for books over 130 pages
- must have a 0.0625" clearance or variance (no part of any glyph) to each fold line: nothing goes inside the colored margins

Some of following illustrations use the old cover template colors: red for the bleed/trim zone, and blue for the no-text zone. Most of those pages illustrate interior pages, where the no-text zone remains 0.25" and the need to see the two different zones is important.

CS's Interior Templates, set in Word, do not show the no-text zone, and are not designed for bleed images—although they can be used for them. Other than the specific differences between covers and interior pages (the physical differences, all covers bleed four sides, and the size of the no-text/no-live element zone), how to have elements bleed or not bleed and what CS will accept or reject are basically the same. The do's and dont's in the following pages would apply to cover and interior files; the only exceptions are two-page, interior, images which have their own issues.

Note: CS will add 1 or 2 leaves (2 or 4 pages) at the end of each book. The last page will include a barcode, with date and place of manufacture.

---

* This inner zone has had several names: title-safe zone, no-live element zone, out-of-live zone, and I call it the no-text zone. Given CS's idiosyncratic definition of "live element," no-live element zone is probably best.

† Each template is designed to fit your total page count plus or minus within a ten-page range: for example, the ranges are 161-170 pages, 291-300 pages, 311-320 pages . . . The download file name will be, for example, *BookCover6x9_Color_300.zip*; that is, CS uses the same zip file for 292 to 300 page interiors. The actual template will say, in this case, "294.0 page" (always the file name number less 6), because that size/page count is used to create the template.

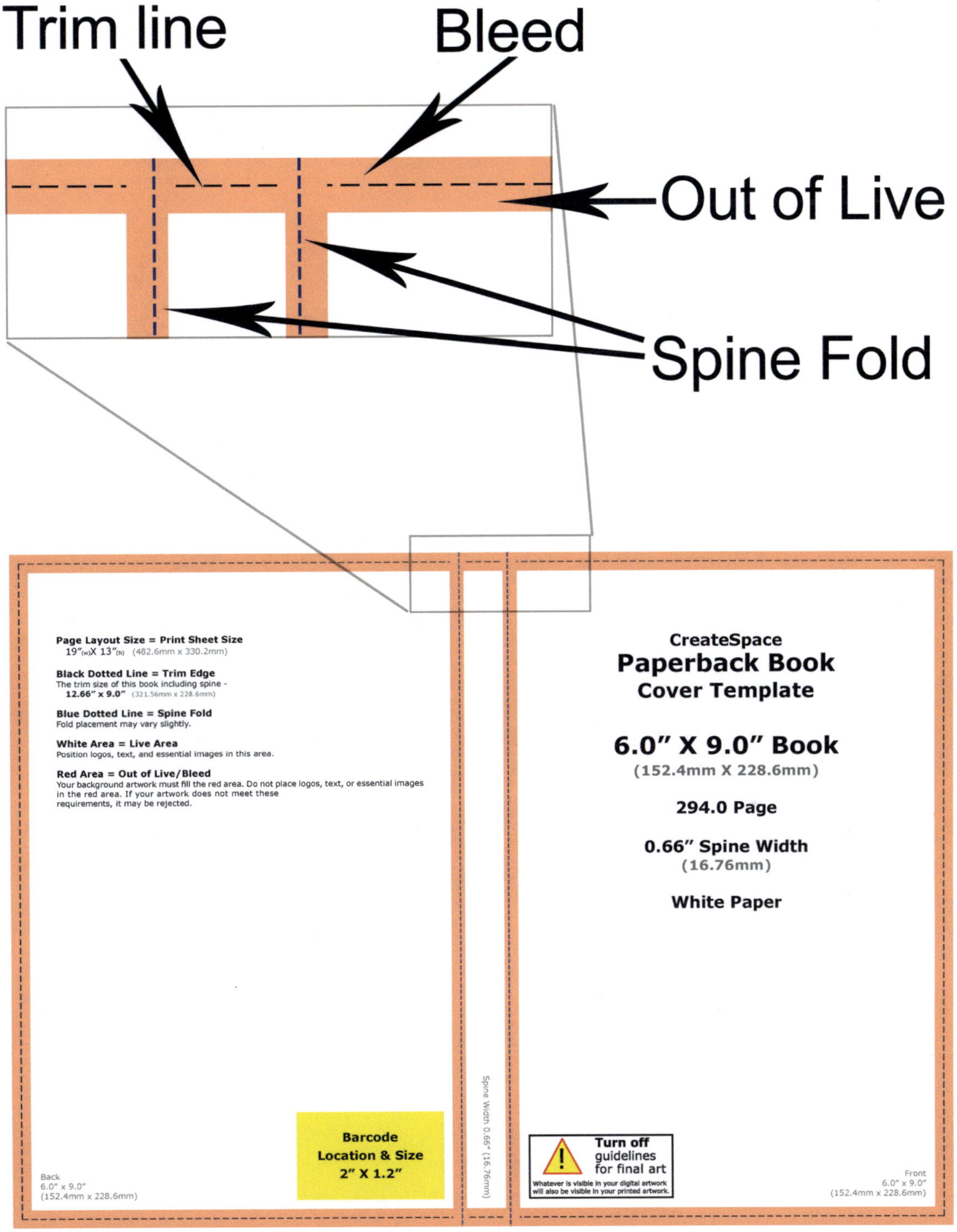
Trim line
Bleed
Out of Live
Spine Fold
Page Layout Size = Print Sheet Size
19"(w)X 13"(h) (482.6mm x 330.2mm)
Black Dotted Line = Trim Edge
The trim size of this book including spine -
12.66" x 9.0" (321.56mm x 228.6mm)
Blue Dotted Line = Spine Fold
Fold placement may vary slightly.
White Area = Live Area
Position logos, text, and essential images in this area.
Red Area = Out of Live/Bleed
Your background artwork must fill the red area. Do not place logos, text, or essential images in the red area. If your artwork does not meet these requirements, it may be rejected.
Back
6.0" x 9.0"
(152.4mm x 228.6mm)
Barcode
Location & Size
2" X 1.2"
Spine Width 0.66" (16.76mm)
CreateSpace
Paperback Book
Cover Template
6.0" X 9.0" Book
(152.4mm X 228.6mm)
294.0 Page
0.66" Spine Width
(16.76mm)
White Paper
Turn off
guidelines
for final art
Whatever is visible in your digital artwork will also be visible in your printed artwork.
Front
6.0" x 9.0"
(152.4mm x 228.6mm)

Recommended Cover Margins: This is the same basic template as on the previous page, but with one big difference—the creases left during binding are indicated. On some books there are no marks, but on most books the marks are quite obvious. I believe the crease is a bruise left by the clamping device used to affix the cover during binding. It is parallel to the edge of the spine, and is approximately 0.25″ in from it. See below.

Although you can use the 0.125″, if your text is too close to the spine, the crease will run through the letters. If this happens it looks like a mistake.

For safety, I would recommend staying inside the trim line by a 0.25″: along the spine to avoid the crease, and for symmetry as well as safety along the outside, top, and bottom edges.

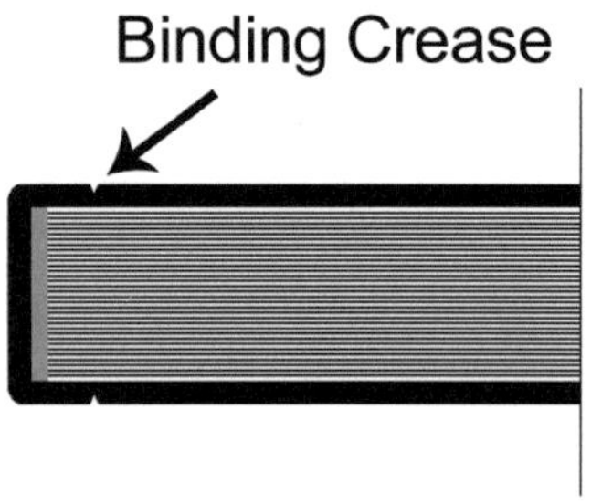

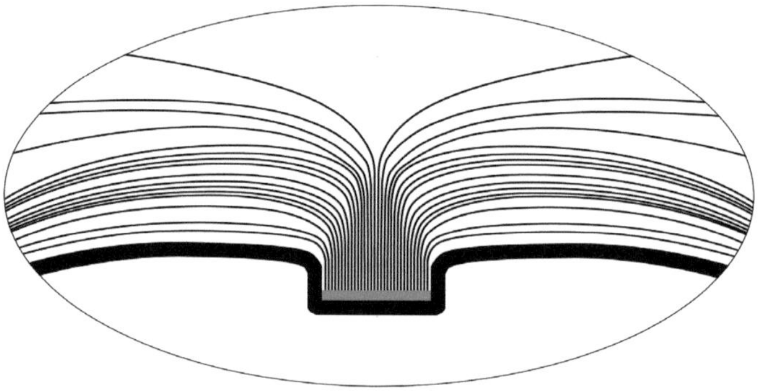

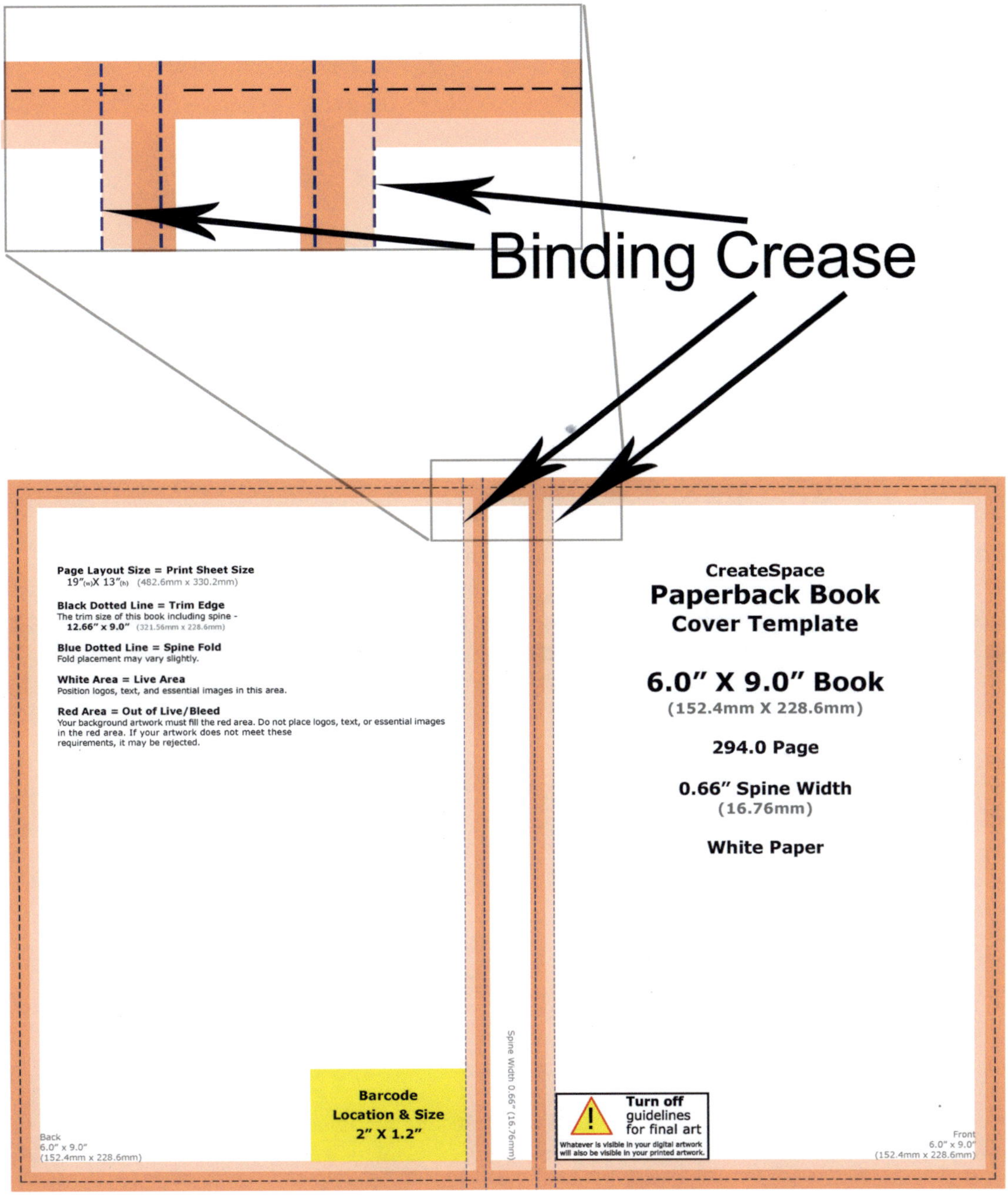
Binding Crease
Page Layout Size = Print Sheet Size
19"(w)X 13"(h) (482.6mm x 330.2mm)
Black Dotted Line = Trim Edge
The trim size of this book including spine -
12.66" x 9.0" (321.56mm x 228.6mm)
Blue Dotted Line = Spine Fold
Fold placement may vary slightly.
White Area = Live Area
Position logos, text, and essential images in this area.
Red Area = Out of Live/Bleed
Your background artwork must fill the red area. Do not place logos, text, or essential images in the red area. If your artwork does not meet these requirements, it may be rejected.
Barcode
Location & Size
2" X 1.2"
Back
6.0" x 9.0"
(152.4mm x 228.6mm)
Spine Width 0.66" (16.76mm)
CreateSpace
Paperback Book
Cover Template
6.0" X 9.0" Book
(152.4mm X 228.6mm)
294.0 Page
0.66" Spine Width
(16.76mm)
White Paper
Turn off
guidelines
for final art
Whatever is visible in your digital artwork will also be visible in your printed artwork.
Front
6.0" x 9.0"
(152.4mm x 228.6mm)

Cover Templates & backgrounds—DIY: Cover templates only come in certain sizes. If your trim size is non-standard, build your own book cover template. See page 7-9 for the specification.

Most graphics programs have rulers, a measuring tool, and guidelines that can be dragged into place. Calculate the overall size of the cover plus bleed. Create a new file at that size and at 300 dpi. Indicate the bleed, the out-of-live margins, spine, etc, with guidelines. Your template should resemble the following page, or with guidelines. The dotted line indicates the outside dimensions of the cover along the very edge of the bleed.

You will build your cover from the bottom up, using separate layers, see pages 26-27.

In every graphics program I have worked with, the guidelines are non-printing: so you do not have to worry about them showing up on your cover.

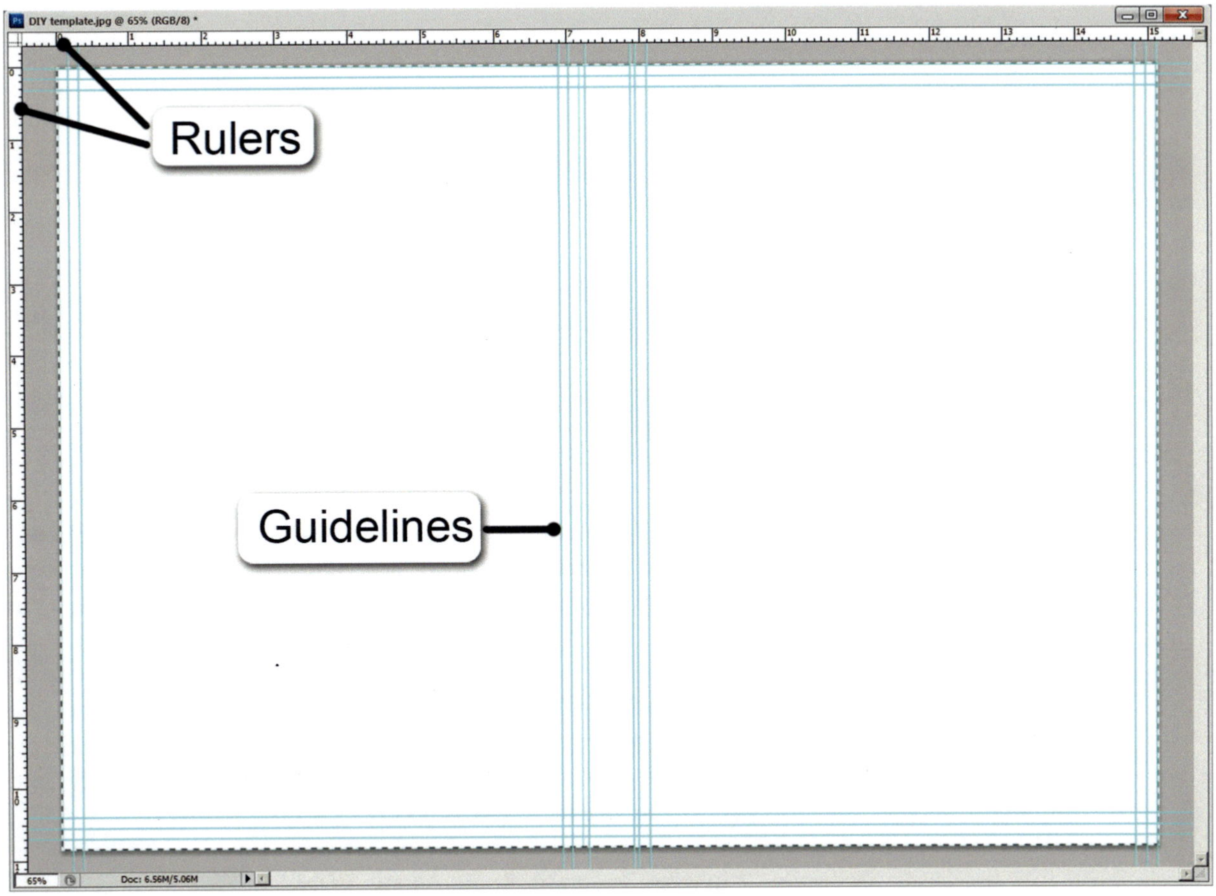
DIY template.jpg @ 65% (RGB/8) *
Rulers
Guidelines
65%
Doc: 6.56M/5.06M

Cover Templates: The following example shows a cover being assembled using seven layers, with the new template.

The least number of layers would be one: if you did not use a template, and simply put put text over white, as in a word processor. Most word processors will let you place an image or background and put text directly over it. Although these are not called layers, they are in effect two layers, text and image.*

This cover shows transparency (the checkerboard backgrounds seen in the layers palette). When this cover is finished, a good workflow would be to save it so that all the layers are preserved: generally in the programs native format. Then a copy would be flattened (all the layers merged into one layer and any invisible layers thrown out. This could be saved as a JPG or a TIFF file.

TIFF files are larger and are a little more accurate. Some people complain that JPGs soften the ISBN barcode too much. My experience is that it doesn't have to, but it is not difficult to examine the barcode under magnification.

If the PDF converts to JPG (PDFs save images as JPGs or TIFFs), which is a typical default setting even for PDF/X-1a, then make sure the barcode is sharp. Some programs accept vector images, which are like type in that they are "infinitely" scalable. A standard format for vector barcodes is EPS.

- Bottom image is the Template only.
- The middle image is the Cover Art and the Template, which is partially hidden by the Cover Art, only the white background shows.
- The top image shows all the text, Barcode white, and ISBN Barcodes layers on.

Note: In the top image, none of the colored part of the template is showing. If any of it showed, the cover art would be incorrect.

---

* Word, for example, uses layers (background, text, images, etc.), but they are not accessed as layers as they are in most graphics programs, nor is there as much control over them.

A Book of Koan
John Doe, editor
A Book of Koan John Doe, editor

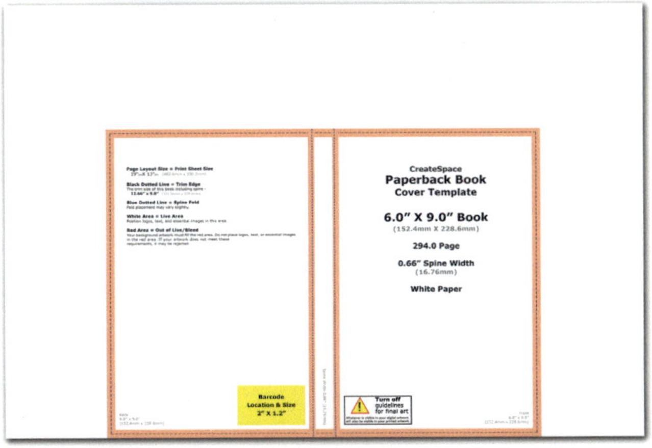
CreateSpace
Paperback Book
Cover Template
6.0" X 9.0" Book
(152.4mm X 228.6mm)
294.0 Page
0.66" Spine Width
(16.76mm)
White Paper
Barcode
Location & Size
2" X 1.2"
Turn off
guidelines
for final art

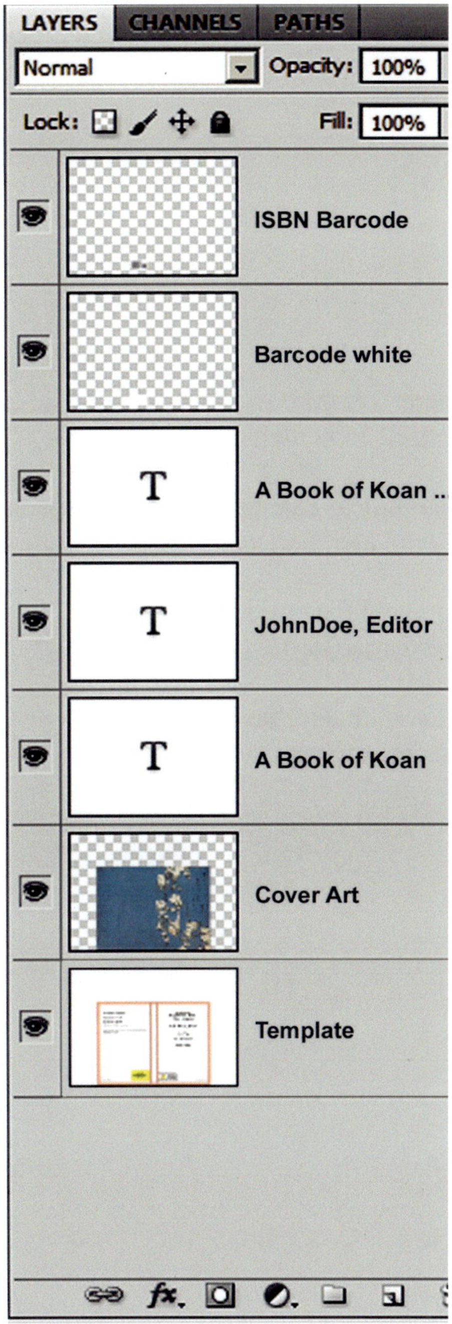
LAYERS
CHANNELS
PATHS
Normal
Opacity: 100%
Lock:
Fill: 100%
ISBN Barcode
Barcode white
A Book of Koan ...
JohnDoe, Editor
A Book of Koan
Cover Art
Template

Cover Templates: when a cover is white, and with no crop marks, it is difficult to assess if the art is sized correctly without measuring

The middle example could be misjudged and changed by CS, which has happened recently to several members who submitted white covers on the full template background.

To avoid the cover being changed, I recommend cropping it exactly to size, which includes the bleed area (top).

A drop shadow has been added to assist in seeing the white template and cover: do not add a drop shadow to your cover art.

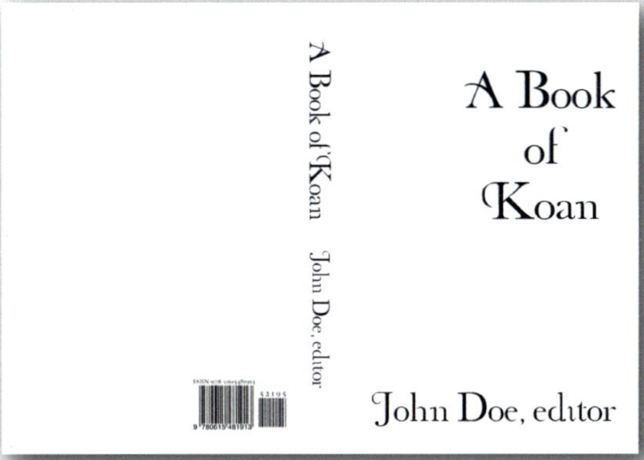
A Book of Koan
John Doe, editor
A Book of Koan John Doe, editor

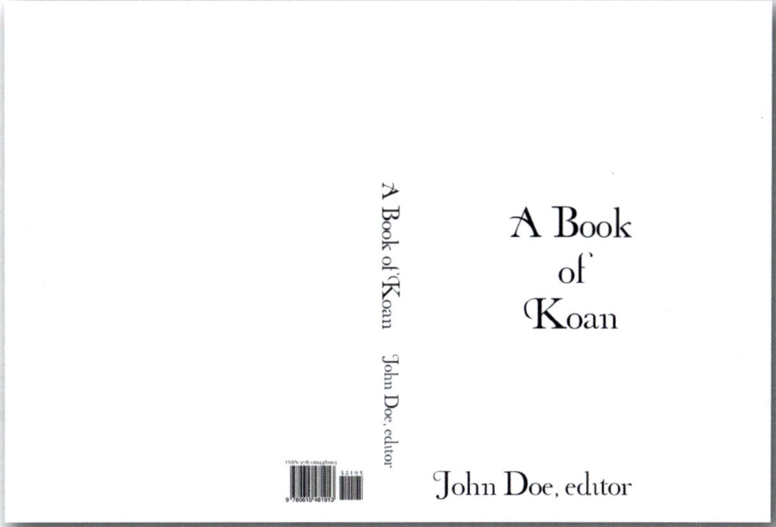
A Book of Koan
John Doe, editor
A Book of Koan John Doe, editor

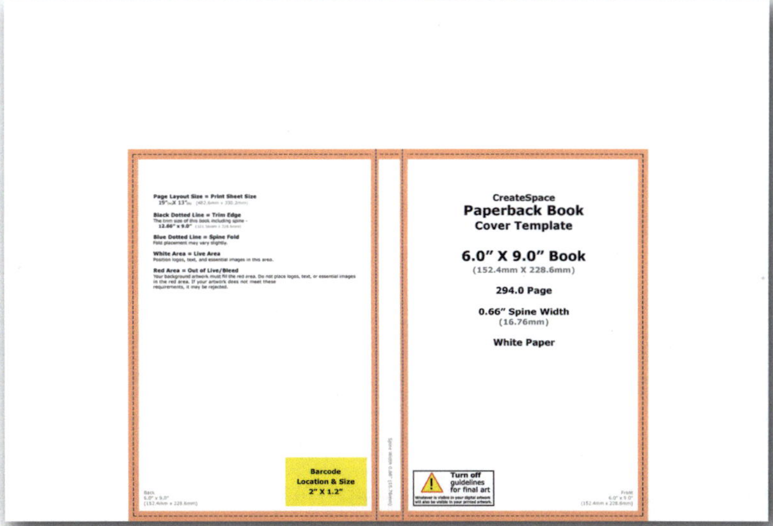
CreateSpace
Paperback Book
Cover Template
6.0" X 9.0" Book
(152.4mm X 228.6mm)
294.0 Page
0.66" Spine Width
(16.76mm)
White Paper
Barcode
Location & Size
2" X 1.2"
Turn off guidelines for final art

Page Margins: Aside from the inner margin, the minimum size of which depends on the book's page count, see page 9, every page has two margins that must be observed. These margins are the same regardless of the page or trim size. Using CS's names:

Title Safe Zone (on cover) or *No-live Element Zone,* or *Out-of-Live*—this is a 0.25" margin.* No text may encroach it. No image may be partially in it. Early templates show this as blue.

Trim area (bleed)—this is a minimum 0.125" area that extends beyond the trim line.

Covers—all covers print in color, and all covers are presumed to bleed, even if they don't. That is, the dimensions must include a bleed, even if no image or background color actually bleeds. Text cannot bleed.

Interior pages—if one side of one page has a bleed, the book interior is listed as a bleed. Thus if your trim size is 6" x 9" the actual page size of your PDF (all pages) must be 6.125" x 9.25".

If you use a cover template, it may use these colors if it is old and the inner title-safe zone will be shown 0.25", or just red if it is new and the title-safe zone will be shown as 0.125". Normally, the template is disposable. The colors are a convenience.

* As noted on the previous pages, this margin has changed for covers: 0.625″ on the spine, 0.125″ along the outside edges of the front and back covers.

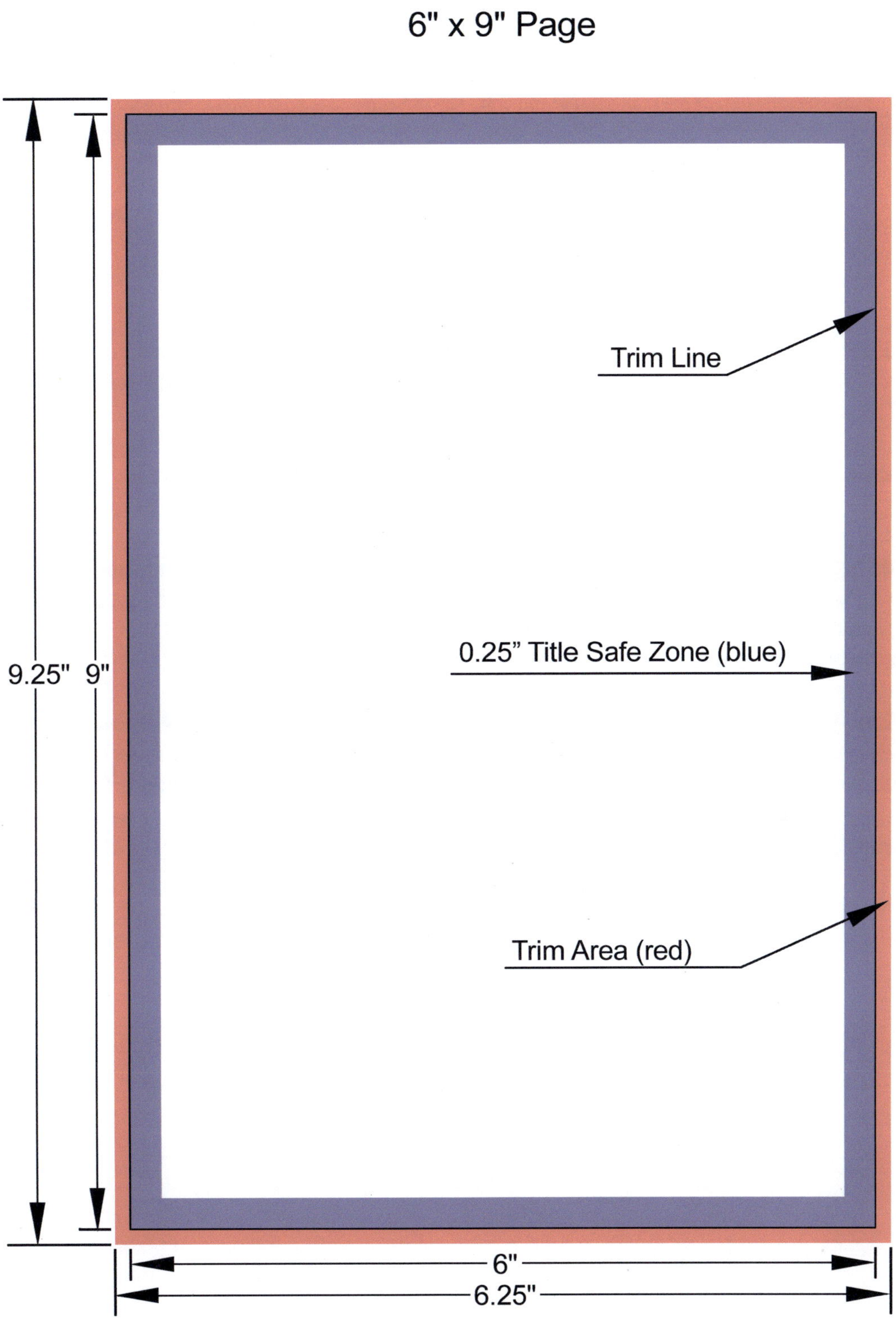
6" x 9" Page
Trim Line
0.25" Title Safe Zone (blue)
Trim Area (red)
9.25"
9"
6"
6.25"

Bleeds—single page images: Ignoring the inner margin, if you want an image or background color to extend to the very edge of the paper, which has to be trimmed, the image must extend beyond the edge. The image must bleed.

An image does not have to bleed on all sides, it could bleed just off the top, or bottom, or outside.

A single-page picture that appears to bleed off the inside edge can either be constructed with a bleed on the inside edge or without: see pages 38-41 for an illustration of 2-page bleeds. It is unclear what specific policies or procedures CS uses for this. I would create the book as a bleed just to be safe. My preference is to have the image end flush with the inside edge of the page: and like the 2-page image, this leaves a white strip, which is basically invisible.

The Trim Line is the edge of the sheet where it is trimmed. If all goes right, it will look like the following example (lower right corner). When the book's pages are gathered they must be jogged, the spine of the cover is glued to the spine edge of the interior page, it is clamped, folded and trimmed. The bleed or trim area is insurance that if things are off a little there won't be a sliver of white, unprinted, paper showing along an edge. Printers typically ask for a bleed of 0.125″ to 0.25″.

The following image bleeds four sides (4S).

6" x 9" Page

Bleeds: Whether it's an image, a background, or a graphic element, if it bleeds it must extend all the way through the 0.25" no-text zone, across the trim line, and at least to the outer edge of the trim area.

Here it is two decorative lines under the header that bleed.

This page bleeds on one side (1S), and even if this were the only bleed, you must add 0.125" to the top and bottom as well as the bleed side. (See instructions on previous spread.)

Material can bleed on any side.

6" x 9" Page

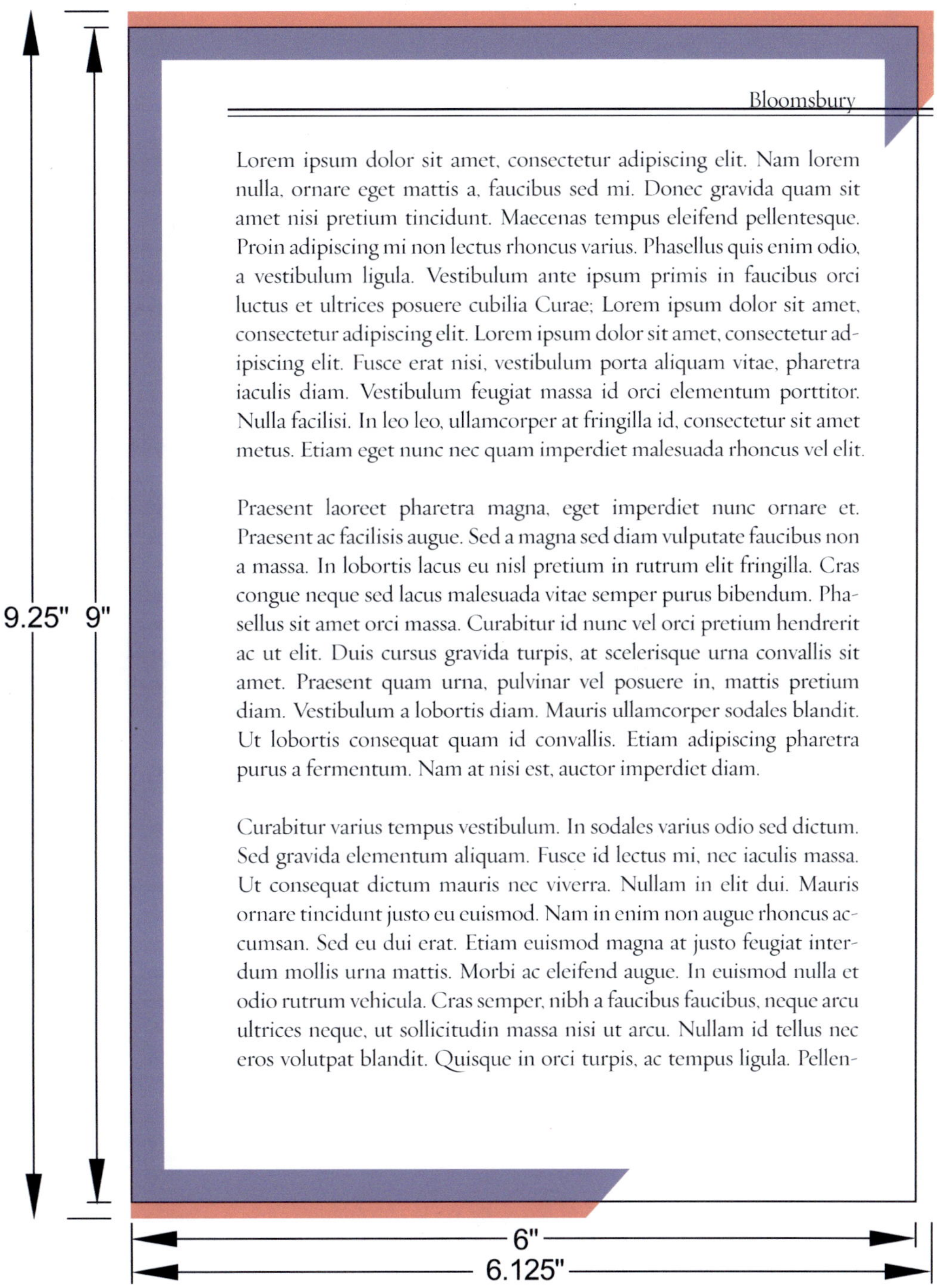
9.25"
9"
Bloomsbury
Lorem ipsum dolor sit amet, consectetur adipiscing elit. Nam lorem nulla, ornare eget mattis a, faucibus sed mi. Donec gravida quam sit amet nisi pretium tincidunt. Maecenas tempus eleifend pellentesque. Proin adipiscing mi non lectus rhoncus varius. Phasellus quis enim odio, a vestibulum ligula. Vestibulum ante ipsum primis in faucibus orci luctus et ultrices posuere cubilia Curae; Lorem ipsum dolor sit amet, consectetur adipiscing elit. Lorem ipsum dolor sit amet, consectetur adipiscing elit. Fusce erat nisi, vestibulum porta aliquam vitae, pharetra iaculis diam. Vestibulum feugiat massa id orci elementum porttitor. Nulla facilisi. In leo leo, ullamcorper at fringilla id, consectetur sit amet metus. Etiam eget nunc nec quam imperdiet malesuada rhoncus vel elit.
Praesent laoreet pharetra magna, eget imperdiet nunc ornare et. Praesent ac facilisis augue. Sed a magna sed diam vulputate faucibus non a massa. In lobortis lacus eu nisl pretium in rutrum elit fringilla. Cras congue neque sed lacus malesuada vitae semper purus bibendum. Phasellus sit amet orci massa. Curabitur id nunc vel orci pretium hendrerit ac ut elit. Duis cursus gravida turpis, at scelerisque urna convallis sit amet. Praesent quam urna, pulvinar vel posuere in, mattis pretium diam. Vestibulum a lobortis diam. Mauris ullamcorper sodales blandit. Ut lobortis consequat quam id convallis. Etiam adipiscing pharetra purus a fermentum. Nam at nisi est, auctor imperdiet diam.
Curabitur varius tempus vestibulum. In sodales varius odio sed dictum. Sed gravida elementum aliquam. Fusce id lectus mi, nec iaculis massa. Ut consequat dictum mauris nec viverra. Nullam in elit dui. Mauris ornare tincidunt justo eu euismod. Nam in enim non augue rhoncus accumsan. Sed eu dui erat. Etiam euismod magna at justo feugiat interdum mollis urna mattis. Morbi ac eleifend augue. In euismod nulla et odio rutrum vehicula. Cras semper, nibh a faucibus faucibus, neque arcu ultrices neque, ut sollicitudin massa nisi ut arcu. Nullam id tellus nec eros volutpat blandit. Quisque in orci turpis, ac tempus ligula. Pellen-
6"
6.125"

Bleeds: (Excluding the inner margin, which doesn't exist here) nothing on this either bleeds or violates the margins.* If all the pages in the interior are like this, do not select Bleed when uploading your book: it would not bleed.

In the interior upload window, you must select whether the book bleeds or not. If nothing bleeds, select *Ends* ***before*** *the edge of the page*; however, even if only one thing bleeds, then the entire book is set as a bleed—select *Ends* ***after*** *the edge of the page.*

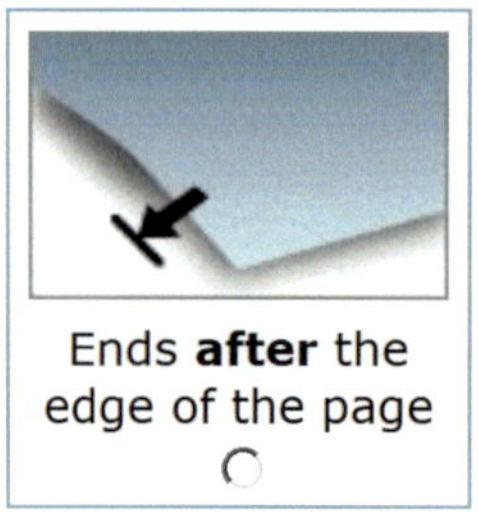

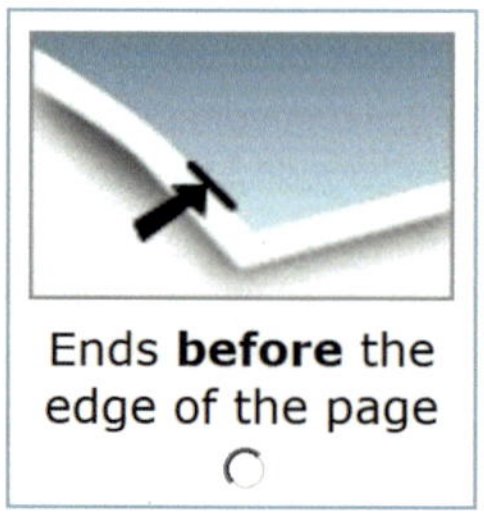

Right: *Mother of Egypt,* by Walton Mendelson

* In practice, however, there would be a minimum inner margin (see chart on page 9), based on the page count of the book. Of course, the margins can be bigger than the minimums.

6" x 9" Page

Mother of Egypt

Created in 2004, this was the first of series of narrative studies where there was a central figure. All of these figures are classic in nature, some heroic like Psyche or the Madonna, others such as *Homeless*, center on a figure of pathos, who, nonetheless, struggles to act heroically. These lead, interestingly to the

9"

6"

2-Page Images: Here the image appears to "bleed" across the spine. Done this way, the pages do not bleed, and the image is split in half, positioned carefully, so that it would line up exactly from one page to the next. (A single page image can be treated this way.)

Note, if you cannot work in spreads because your program does not show them correctly (here pages 16-17), remember that the left hand pages is the even numbered page (verso), and the right hand page is the odd numbered page (recto).

The image is exactly split in half. (If you wanted an asymmetrical bleed, more on one page than the other, your workflow would be the same.)

When these pages print, there will be a white strip of up to 0.125″ on each page. I did a 42 page art book in which every page was completely black. Formatted this way, although there was a white strip, it was not visible unless the books were mashed down, and even then it was barely noticeable.

When working in InDesign, the image is placed whole and intact in position on the facing pages. When the image is converted to PDF, InDesign splits the image.

This and the following process can be done in programs other than InDesign. But planning and a very careful workflow are vital.

Note:

This is for interiors only.

This 2-page image does not actually bleed in the sense that the image does not extend past the edge of inside edge of the pages. However, for CS to process this, the book must be set up as a bleed. According to Technical Support, this is an issue with color but not black and white books. However, it is advisable to treat black and white books the same way:

- set them up as bleeds
- apply a bleed (adding 0.125″ to the top, outside, and bottom) of the trim size.

Right: *Monument Valley* by Walton Mendelson

6" x 9" Page
6" x 9" Page
9"
9"
[16]
[17]
6"
6"

[16]
[17]

2-Page Images: Here the image bleeds across the spine. However, unlike the preceding example, this is a bleed, and the book interior will bleed. (A single page image can be treated this way.)

The image is split in half plus 0.125". (If you wanted an asymmetrical bleed, more on one page than the other, your workflow would be the same.) Thus the trim areas overlap from one side to the other. When the book is trimmed, this overlapping excess is trimmed away. The examples I've seen have a slight jump between the two sections: but this isn't noticeable in the actual book, just as the white strip in the preceding example is rarely noticeable.

If you cannot work in spreads because your program does not show them correctly, remember that the left hand pages are the even numbered pages (verso), and the right hand pages are the odd numbered pages (recto).

This method is used by Michelle Lovi, http://www.odysseybooks.com.au: She works with InDesign, a desktop publishing program, which lets her place the image—whole and in one piece—in position while working in spreads (facing pages). InDesign honors the mirrored margins, and when the PDF is created and the bleeds are applied, it automatically splits the image.

(If camera ready work were submitted to a traditional non-digital offset printer for an image that bleeds across the spine, this is how it would be handled by the prep department: they would split the image with an overlapping bleed, which, when printed and trimmed, would ideally line up the two sections seamlessly as one single image.)

CS accepts and prints pages configured this way. *Note: as of this fall, however, Michelle has had clients' books altered when 2-page images were created this way. This does not appear to be a change in policy, only that some CS people think this is incorrect and take it upon themselves to fix it*

See the note on page 38.

Right: *Faithful Apostles* by Walton Mendelson

6" x 9" Page
9.25"
9"
[24]
6"
6.25"
6" x 9" Page
9.25"
9"
[25]
6"
6.25"

[24]
[25]

Bleeds: Bleeds and margin errors account for many of the file rejections by CS.

Top: Typical Problems—Examples of what will cause a file to be rejected

A. The image extends into (but not through) the 0.25″ out-of-live zone: *Note—here the offending sliver of image is visible, but it could also be a white border—i.e. non-printing—that is part of the image and that would cause the book to be rejected.*

B. Text extends into the 0.25″ out-of-live zone, even it is intended to.

C. Text on an image (albeit Japanese) that extends into the out-of-live zone. *Note—any character from any language in a picture, even though it is simply in the background as a sign or the label on a box—something irrelevant to the image—is considered text (a live element) by CS.*

D. A graphic element that bleeds, but not to the full 0.125″ required.

E. Text extends into the inner margin.

F. Text extends into the 0.25″ out-of-live zone.

G. Text extends into the out-of-live zone.

H. A letter is split across the spine.

Bottom: Examples of A-H fixed.

A. Moved the image in so the left edge was even with or just in from the 0.25″ margin.

B. Moved the text in so that the far right edge was inside the 0.25″ margin.

C. Moved the text (Japanese kanji is text even though it functions as a decorative element).

D. Extended the green bar to the outside edge of the bleed.

E. Reset the text to fit between the inner margin and the outer, 0.25″ margin.

F. Reset the text to fit between the inner margin and the outer, 0.25″ margin.

G. Divided the picture so that no text was inside the out-of-live zone (0.25″).

H. Divided the picture so that no text letters were split or inside the out-of-live zone (0.25″).

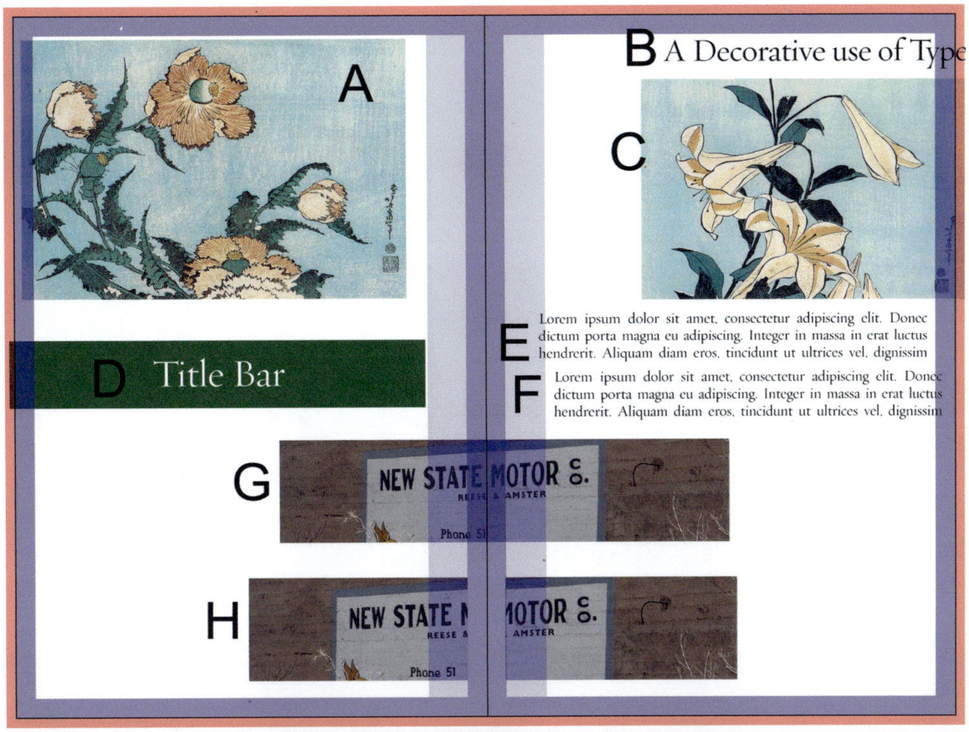

Problems

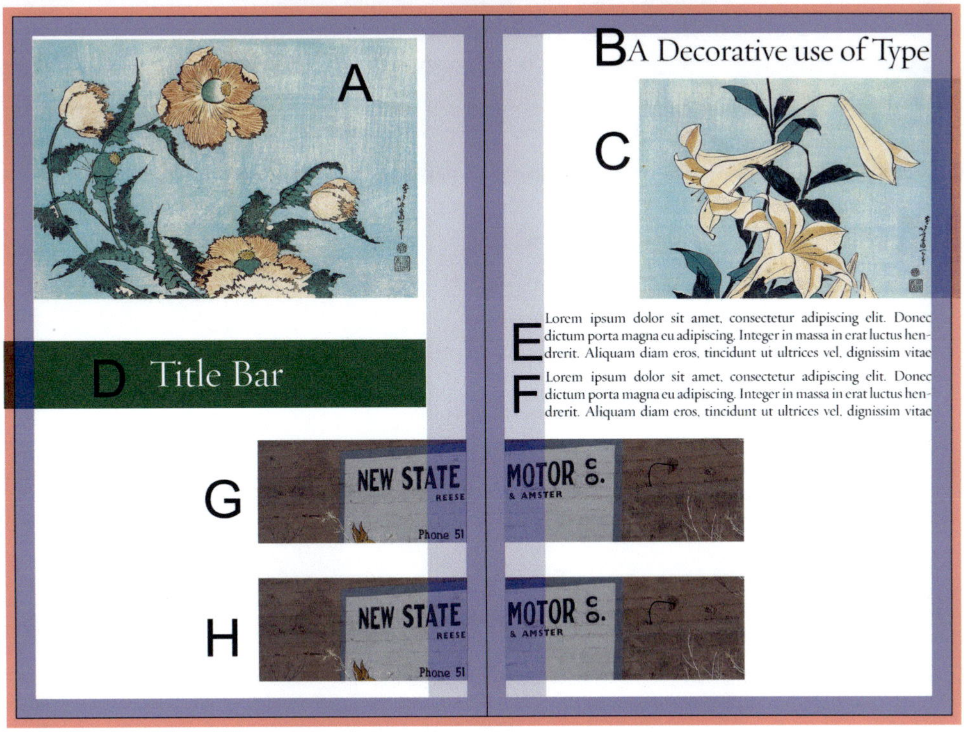

Fixed

Margins: these are very easy to understand as long as there are no pictures that bleed. See page 7–10 for the actual guidelines.

Because the binding is tight (see page 22), CS requires that the inner margins be increased depending on the number of pages in the book. To accommodate the tightness, these margins are larger than many books use; however, large inner margins are common in books bound in other ways.

The visual effect of the tight binding is a loss of about 0.25″, so a 0.75″ inner margins will look more like a 0.5″ one.

Although CS insists on a minimum margin of 0.25″on the top, bottom, and outside, and recommends 0.5″, these are minimums, and for most books, somewhat wider margins create an attractive, more open page.

There is no "correct" set of margins. The best way to judge the effectiveness of your choices is to print out pages, especially in spreads, which often means trimming the pages and taping them together.

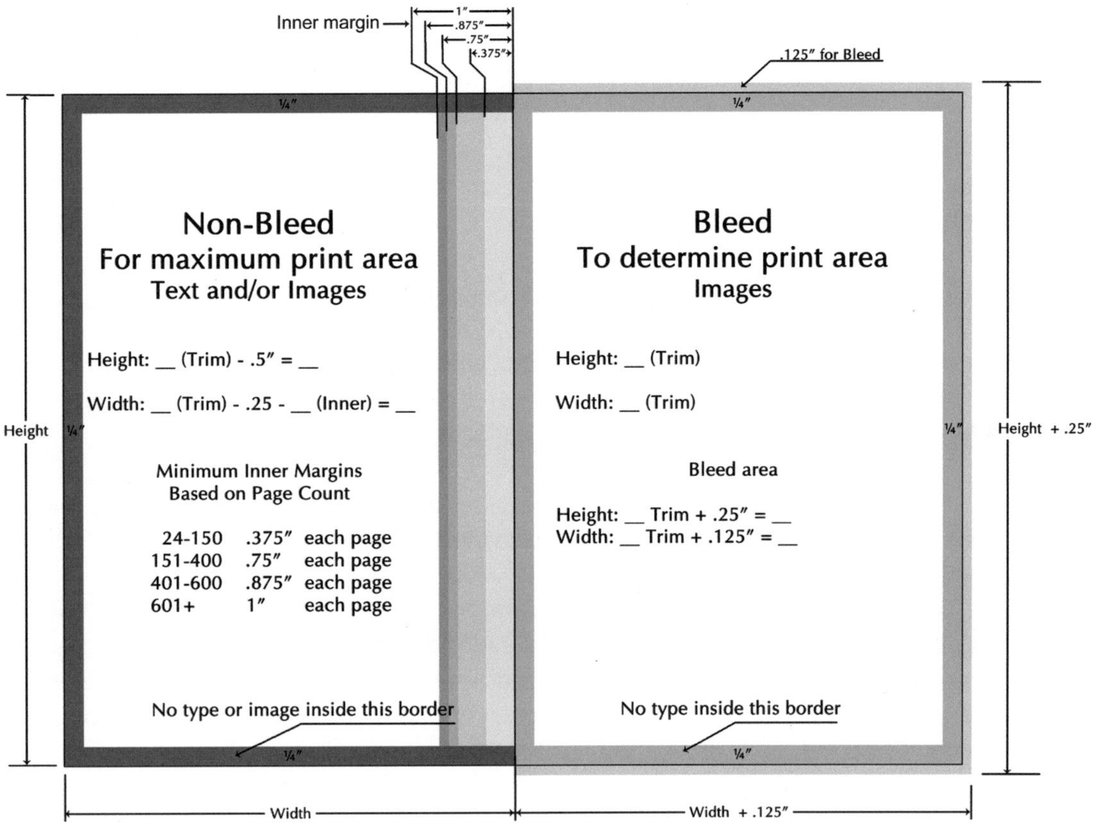
Inner margin
1″
.875″
.75″
.375″
.125″ for Bleed
¼″
¼″
Non-Bleed
For maximum print area
Text and/or Images
Height: __ (Trim) - .5″ = __
Width: __ (Trim) - .25 - __ (Inner) = __
Height
¼″
Minimum Inner Margins
Based on Page Count
24-150 .375″ each page
151-400 .75″ each page
401-600 .875″ each page
601+ 1″ each page
No type or image inside this border
¼″
Width
Bleed
To determine print area
Images
Height: __ (Trim)
Width: __ (Trim)
¼″
Height + .25″
Bleed area
Height: __ Trim + .25″ = __
Width: __ Trim + .125″ = __
No type inside this border
¼″
Width + .125″

Landscape Format

Landscape Books: with the spine/binding on the left, are limited to:

- minimum height 6″
- maximum width: 8.5″

No non-portrait size, except the square 8.5″ x 8.5″ in color, is an Industry Standard.

CS does offer a landscape format using what is often called calender binding: the book is right reading when held horizontally, but the pages turn from bottom to top, with the binding along the top, not the side. Next page: Scenic Calendar and Landscape Book (top)

The contents of the PDF have to be turned 90° CCW, and the PDF oriented as a book in portrait format. The binding will be done along the long, vertical left hand edge of the book, in this orientation. Next page: Front Cover and Interior (bottom).

When the book is then printed, bound, and trimmed and then held right reading, the binding will be at the top of the closed book. When this procedure was developed, CS asked that customers contact Customer Support and notify them that the book was to be *top bound.* I would recommend notifying Customer Support, even though the last time I did it, the Customer Support person had no idea why I was calling, “We can tell from the PDF what you want.” Call to be safe.

The minimum inner margins, out-of-live area, page counts, etc. are the same as those previously described when the book is viewed as it will be printed, PDF Orientation.

Right: *Still Life No. 1, The Death of Arthur, Plutus Contemplates Abundance,* and *Zorand*, by Walton Mendelson

Scenic Calendar

Landscape Book: Top Bound

Reader's Spreads

Front Cover

Interior

PDF Orientation

Miscellaneous

COLOR

Most digital art is produced in sRGB, but CS and most other printers print in CMYK. CS prints well from RGB work, converting it to CMYK. Most full color scenes will look perceptually correct: all the colors will be modified to maintain their relationships to each other.

CS uses non-traditional process colors (redder magenta, stronger cyan, richer black) and proprietary profiles, to better emulate sRGB color.

Although bright, saturated colors in RGB will be dull and flat in CMYK, they will be perceptually correct in relation to other colors, so they should not stand out. However, if your work has large areas of these colors (called out-of-gamut colors), then you need to be aware of that and possibly adjust your work accordingly.

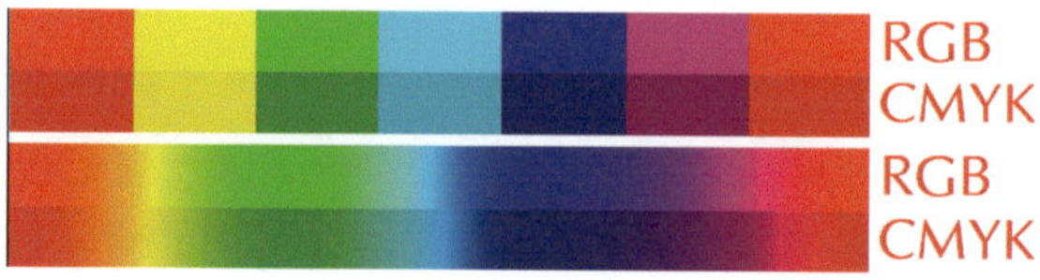

Some people avoid this problem by working in CMYK or with CMYK colors from the start, but not all graphics programs permit this (e.g. Photoshop and Corel Painter do—GIMP, Elements, and PaintShopPro do not). Other people, if the work is critical, will convert sRGB to CMYK themselves and color correct it for print.

The ideal and requested image resolution (the number of image pixels per inch) is 300—commonly stated as 300 dpi (dots per inch), although ppi would be more correct.

CS can print 400% total ink coverage (TIC)—that is, 100% of each color. However, as the TIC moves above 250% or so, while it will print, the colors/image areas (shadow detail) become deep, dark, and muddy. Most monitors are too bright, so colors above 250% probably stand out with reasonable separation, but not in print.

Your desktop inkjet printer is CMYK. Print out all or at least some of your images. They will have been converted to CMYK and they will not be as bright as your monitor. *Printing your images will answer a lot of questions.*

If you are particularly worried about printing images, make a test book: 24 page minimum, free ISBN, throw-away title, simple white cover with text (unless you are testing the cover too) put in images with descriptive text so you know what you've done. Delivered in the US, this will cost less than $10.

BARCODES

Barcodes: If you place your own barcode on the cover, it can be colors other than black on white, and it does not have to be in the lower right corner. See:
www.barcode-us.com/upc/upsColorChart.html —color
www.isbn.org/standards/home/isbn/international/html/usm7.htm —printing
www.terryburton.co.uk/barcodewriter/generator/ —free barcodes

Made in the USA
Monee, IL
09 November 2026

67971940R00031